CORE KNOWLEDGE LIBRARY

TEACHER'S GUIDE
GRADE 2

Photo Credits: p. 7: tr: © LLC, FogStock/Index Open; p. 10 lc: James Levin/Studio 10/ SODA, c: © Masterfile, rc: © Image 100/SODA, bl: © VStock/Index Open, bc: © EyeWire, Inc./Photodisc Collection/Getty Images, br: James Levin © Scholastic Inc.

No part of this publication may be reproduced in whole or in part, or stored in a retrieval system, or transmitted in any form or by any means, electronic, mechanical, photocopying, recording, or otherwise, without written permission of the publisher. For information regarding permission, write to Scholastic Inc., 557 Broadway, New York, NY 10012.

Acknowledgments and credits appear on pages 29–32, which constitute an extension of this copyright page.

Copyright © 2006 Scholastic Inc.
All rights reserved.   Published by Scholastic Inc.   Printed in the U.S.A.

ISBN:0-439-86253-1

SCHOLASTIC, ROOKIE BIOGRAPHIES, ROOKIE READ-ABOUT, and associated logos and designs are trademarks and/or registered trademarks of Scholastic Inc.
CORE KNOWLEDGE is a registered trademark of The Core Knowledge Foundation.
Other company names, brand names, and product names are the property and/or trademarks of their respective owners.

1 2 3 4 5 6 7 8 9 10 40   15 14 13 12 11 10 09 08 07 06

CONTENTS

E. D. Hirsch, Jr. 4

Letter From E.D. Hirsch, Jr. 5

What is Core Knowledge? 6

Overview of the *Core Knowledge Sequence, Grades K–2* 8

The Core Knowledge Classroom Library 10
    Overview 10
    How the Books Were Selected 11
    Setting Up and Using the Library 12

The Books in the Grade 2 Library 13
    Language Arts/English 13
    History & Geography 15
    Visual Arts 18
    Music 20
    Mathematics 20
    Science 22

About the Core Knowledge Foundation

E. D. Hirsch, Jr.

E. D. Hirsch, Jr. is the author of ten books, including the best-sellers *Cultural Literacy, The Schools We Need and Why We Don't Have Them,* and *The Dictionary of Cultural Literacy.* Other books written or edited by E. D. Hirsch on topics related to education include *The First Dictionary of Cultural Literacy*; the Core Knowledge Series: *What Your Kindergartner – Sixth Grader Needs to Know*; and *The Knowledge Deficit.* These works have influenced recent educational thought and practice in the United States and other countries.

Hirsch began his teaching career at Yale, specializing in Romantic Poetry and Literary Theory. In 1966 he became Professor of English at the University of Virginia, where he served twice as chairman of his department. During his academic career he authored several books on literary theory as well as studies on Blake and Wordsworth. At the time of his retirement from the University of Virginia in 2002, he was University Professor of Education and Humanities, holding positions both in the College of Arts and Sciences and in the Curry School of Education.

From the mid 80s on, Hirsch has devoted himself to the mission of educational reform, principally in American elementary schools. He has concentrated his efforts on developing a curriculum that provides coherence and rich content in the foundational years of a child's education. In 1986 he established the Core Knowledge® Foundation in Charlottesville, Virginia, to design this curriculum and support its implementation. In developing the curriculum, the framework of which is presented in the book, *The Core Knowledge Sequence: Content Guidelines K–8*, he enlisted the help of hundreds of teachers and specialists in language arts, history, geography, science, math, and the fine arts.

Professor Hirsch is a graduate of Cornell University and holds masters and doctorate degrees from Yale University, as well as several honorary degrees. In 1977 he was elected to the American Academy of Arts and Sciences and in 1996 to the International Academy of Education. He has been a Fulbright and a Guggenheim Fellow, a fellow of the Center for Advanced Study in the Behavioral Sciences at Stanford University, a Humanities Fellow at Princeton University, a fellow at the Australian National University, and an honoree of the Royal Dutch Academy. In 2003 he was honored with one of two "Excellence in Education" prizes awarded for the first time by the Fordham Foundation of Dayton, Ohio.

Dear Educator,

No ability in our modern world is more important than reading comprehension. For children who can read and understand, America really is a land of opportunity. But for those who cannot read—or cannot make sense of what they read—opportunities are vastly reduced.

All good readers share two important qualities. First, they have the ability to sound out the words on the page rapidly and effortlessly, and second, they have an extensive body of knowledge to draw on that helps them comprehend the words they are sounding out. Good readers know key events and people from history. They understand important principles of science and mathematics. They recognize idioms, phrases, and allusions. They have an extensive vocabulary and a wide knowledge of the world. In short, they possess what I call "cultural literacy."

It is my belief that children of all socioeconomic backgrounds can become good readers if they have opportunities to learn the foundational knowledge that is most essential for reading comprehension. That body of knowledge is outlined in the *Core Knowledge Sequence: Content Guidelines K–8*, a document developed by hundreds of scholars, teachers, and concerned citizens.

Over the years teachers have told us that one of the most challenging aspects of teaching the *Core Knowledge Sequence* is finding age-appropriate resources. The pioneers who began teaching the curriculum in the early 1990s had to search for suitable resources. This classroom library is intended to make the search for resources less burdensome by providing a collection of key books in six curriculum areas. A few of the books included in the library have been created under the supervision of staff at the Core Knowledge Foundation; others have been selected by experienced Core Knowledge teachers. All have been selected because we feel they will help you to teach the curriculum and to build cultural literacy among your students. We hope you'll agree that this Core Knowledge Classroom Library is a great way to "share the knowledge."

Sincerely,

E D Hirsch

E. D. Hirsch, Jr.
Chairman, Core Knowledge Foundation
Professor Emeritus, The University of Virginia

What Is Core Knowledge?

A Knowledge-Based Curriculum

Core Knowledge is a school reform movement. It is also a curriculum for Grades Kindergarten through 8. The movement and the curriculum were created collaboratively by thousands of educators working under the guidance of the nonprofit, nonpartisan Core Knowledge Foundation of Charlottesville, Virginia. The Foundation exists to promote excellence and equality in American education.

The development of the Core Knowledge curriculum began with a simple research question: *What can educated Americans be expected to know?* What background knowledge can be taken for granted? Research into this subject conducted by E.D. Hirsch, Jr., with assistance from James Trefil and Joseph Kett, culminated in the book *Cultural Literacy: What Every American Should Know*, the purpose of which was to catalog the shared background knowledge of educated Americans.

The logical next step was to pose the question *What would a school curriculum that imparted shared background knowledge look like?* To answer this question, Hirsch created the Core Knowledge Foundation, which carried out an extensive process of research and consensus-building on the creation of a knowledge-based curriculum for the early grades. This process included:

- analyzing the standards and frameworks of state departments of education and of professional organizations such as the National Council of Teachers of Mathematics;
- cross checking those standards and frameworks against the knowledge and skills specified by the standards of successful educational systems in other countries;
- forming an advisory board on multiculturalism to propose a body of core knowledge of diverse cultural traditions that American children should all share as part of their school-based common culture; and
- working with hundreds of teachers, scholars, and scientists around the country to assimilate these materials into a sequence of instruction.

The result of this work was *The Core Knowledge Sequence*, a detailed outline of specific content to be taught in language arts, history, geography, mathematics, science, music, and the visual arts—a curriculum for students in Grades K–8. This curriculum is currently being used in hundreds of schools across the United States that have made a commitment to a richly academic, carefully sequenced, knowledge-based curriculum.

What Sets the Core Knowledge Curriculum Apart?

As students follow the Core Knowledge curriculum they are exposed to a broad range of historical, scientific, and cultural topics that build on one another and prepare them for later educational success. This exposure to a wide array of subject matter is intended not only to develop background knowledge, or cultural literacy, but also to build strong vocabulary in particular subject areas, or domains. Along with decoding skills and specific background knowledge, a strong vocabulary is now recognized to be absolutely essential for true reading comprehension. The Core Knowledge curriculum is, therefore, the ideal curriculum for increasing students' reading abilities. Because the Core Knowledge curriculum is carefully sequenced, it also eliminates many of the gaps and repetitions that characterize other curricula.

Can Schools Not Currently Following the Core Knowledge Curriculum Benefit From the Core Knowledge Classroom Library?

Absolutely. The books in the Core Knowledge Classroom Library have been carefully chosen to build background knowledge in those domains considered to be most essential to later reading. While the books in these libraries have been aligned to the *Core Knowledge Sequence: Content Guidelines for K–8* (see the alignments listed with the individual titles on pages 13–28), all students will benefit from these libraries. They will gain in subject-area knowledge and, most importantly, they will develop vocabulary essential for later reading success.

To find out more about the Core Knowledge curriculum, visit the Foundation's Web site at **www.coreknowledge.org** or call **1-800-238-3233** to order copies of the following complete guidelines to the curriculum.

Core Knowledge Preschool Sequence: Content and Guidelines for Preschool

Core Knowledge Sequence: Content and Guidelines for Grades K–8

Overview of the *Core Knowledge Sequence*, Grades K–2

Core Knowledge at a Glance: Grades K–2

	Kindergarten	**First Grade**	**Second Grade**
Language Arts/English	I. Reading and Writing II. Poetry III. Fiction IV. Sayings and Phrases	I. Reading and Writing II. Poetry III. Fiction IV. Sayings and Phrases	I. Reading and Writing II. Poetry III. Fiction (Stories; Greek Myths; Greek and Roman Myths) IV. Sayings and Phrases
History & Geography	**World** I. Spatial Sense II. Overview of the Seven Continents **American** I. Geography II. Native Americans III. Early Exploration and Settlement (Columbus, Pilgrims, Independence Day) IV. Presidents, Past and Present V. Symbols and Figures	**World** I. Geography II. Early Civilizations (Mesopotamia, Ancient Egypt, History of World Religions) III. Mexico **American** I. Early People and Civilizations (Maya, Inca, Aztec) II. Early Exploraton and Settlement III. American Revolution IV. Early Exploration of the American West V. Symbols and Figures	**World** I. Geography II. Early Civilizations: Asia (India, China) III. Modern Civilization and Culture: Japan IV. Ancient Greece **American** I. American Government: The Constitution II. War of 1812 III. Westward Expansion IV. Civil War V. Immigration and Citizenship VI. Civil Rights VII. Geography of the Americas VIII. Symbols and Figures
Visual Arts	I. Elements of Art II. Sculpture III. Looking at and Talking About Art	I. Art From Long Ago II. Elements of Art III. Kinds of Pictures: Portrait and Still Life	I. Elements of Art II. Sculpture III. Kinds of Pictures: Landscapes IV. Abstract Art V. Architecture

	Kindergarten	**First Grade**	**Second Grade**
Music	I. Elements of Music II. Listening and Understanding III. Songs	I. Elements of Music II. Listening and Understanding (Composers; Orchestra; Opera; Ballet; Jazz) III. Songs	I. Elements of Music II. Listening and Understanding (Orchestra; Keyboards; Composers) III. Songs
Mathematics	I. Patterns and Classification II. Numbers and Number Sense III. Money IV. Computation V. Measurement VI. Geometry	I. Patterns and Classification II. Numbers and Number Sense III. Money IV. Computation V. Measurement VI. Geometry	I. Numbers and Number Sense II. Fractions III. Money IV. Computation V. Measurement VI. Geometry
Science	I. Plants and Plant Growth II. Animals and Their Needs III. Human Body (Five Senses) IV. Introduction to Magnetism V. Seasons and Weather VI. Taking Care of the Earth VII. Science Biographies	I. Living Things and Their Environments II. Human Body (Body Systems) III. Matter IV. Properties of Matter: Measurement V. Introduction to Electricity VI. Astronomy VII. Earth VIII. Science Biographies	I. Cycles in Nature (Seasonal Cycles; Life Cycles; Water Cycles) II. Insects III. Human Body (Cells; Digestive and Excretory Systems) IV. Magnetism V. Seasons and Weather VI. Simple Machines VII. Science Biographies

©2005 Core Knowledge Foundation

The Core Knowledge Classroom Library

Overview

The Core Knowledge Classroom Libraries for Grades K–8 are collections of superb readings in six key curricular areas:

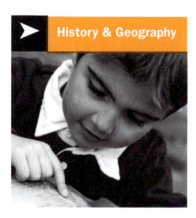

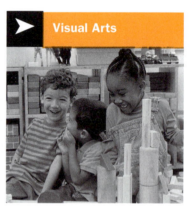

In the past, many elementary school reading programs contained works of fiction exclusively. However, educators now recognize that in order to be successful in today's world, well-read adults must be familiar with a diversity of genres, both fiction and nonfiction. To attain this standard of literacy, students must be given the opportunity to encounter, from the earliest ages, the same sort of diversity in their reading. The purpose of the Core Knowledge Classroom Libraries is to provide this opportunity—to present children with exciting, engaging, knowledge-rich works from across the curriculum—works that will engage them and make them dedicated readers for life.

Selecting Books

How the Books Were Selected

The editors and educators who prepared the lists of books for the Core Knowledge Classroom Libraries made their selections based on the following criteria:

Quality. Each book in these libraries was chosen for the quality of its writing and the fact that it has stood the test of time. Included in the libraries are many recognized classics and works that are destined to become classics.

Scope of Coverage. Books were chosen to cover the whole of the core curriculum for elementary school students and to represent a diversity of genres.

Appropriateness to Level. These books have been chosen to be appropriate to the grade levels to which they have been assigned. As most professionals in elementary education can attest, children's speaking and listening abilities far outpace their reading and writing abilities. Therefore, it is important to read aloud to children as well as to give them opportunities to read independently. The editors have chosen books for these libraries with both purposes in mind. Synopses of the books contained in the Grade 2 Classroom Library can be found on pages 13–28 of this Teacher's Guide. These synopses include suggestions for use, including which books can be read aloud, which can be read independently with assistance from the teacher, and which can be read by the child alone. The editors have chosen books at a range of ability levels to suit these various uses and to provide for some degree of individualization. Teachers may want, for example, to have those students who are exceptional readers attempt to read on their own some of the books identified as appropriate for reading aloud.

Academic Richness. A very important criterion for selection was that the books in these libraries be ones that will build, in each of the curricular areas represented, the essential background knowledge that students need for their future studies. The books in these libraries have been carefully selected to build background knowledge across a diversity of domains of human thought and experience, and thus to develop, over time, reading comprehension.

Richness of Vocabulary. As the National Reading Panel recognized in its landmark report, a key component of reading comprehension is mastery of vocabulary. The works in these libraries have been specifically chosen to build essential reading vocabulary in key semantic domains. Although teachers often think of reading and vocabulary work as two separate activities, it appears that the former is an optimal way of achieving the latter. In that sense, you can think of these classroom libraries, and of knowledge-based curricula in general, as vocabulary-building programs.

Setting Up and Using the Library

Here are some tips for getting the most out of your Core Knowledge Classroom Library.

1 Make the books enticing by displaying them prominently. Make sure that the books are accessible to students, not stuck away on a shelf. Students should be able to rummage and browse through them. Use small easels to display titles related to subjects that you are currently studying as a class.

2 Create reading logs. Keep a reading log, with a page for every student, in your library area. Have your students keep track of the books they've read from the library and from outside the library as well.

3 Have students create reviews and drawings related to the books. Post these on a bulletin board in your library area. This activity helps students to develop ownership of their reading.

4 Store student recommendations with the books. Attach an index card to the inside front cover of each book. Label the index card "Recommended by. . ." and have students who liked the book print their names and give one to five stars to indicate the book's quality. Again, this activity builds ownership.

5 Add books to the library. As you add books to your library, put stars on them and label them with the grade and curricular area (History, Science, Math, etc.). Ask for student recommendations regarding what books should be added.

6 Have students build on their reading. Remember that knowledge builds on knowledge. It's best for students to read and think about a given subject over an extended period of time (several weeks) so that they can build for themselves a knowledge framework about that subject. So, have each student read two or three titles and then choose one of them that he or she really likes. Then have the student do a lot of reading outside the classroom library (in the school or public library and on the Internet) about the subject of that favored book.

7 Keep in your library area a notebook of suggested "Additional Readings" that you and your students build over time. List the title of each book at the top of a page. Then, as you and your students discover additional interesting, related titles, list these under the title of the book in your library. Each page might read, "If you liked [title of book], you will also enjoy. . . ."

The Books in the Grade 2 Library

The Grade 2 Library contains 60 fiction and nonfiction books that support the major categories of the *Core Knowledge Sequence*. The synopses will help you decide how to best use the books with your students and curriculum. Occasionally a book in the library becomes unavailable and another book is substituted. If your library contains a book for which there is no synopsis in this Teacher's Guide, check Scholastic's Web site **www.scholastic.com,** or call customer service at 1-800-724-6527 and we will provide you with one.

Language Arts/English

The Blind Men and the Elephant
retold by Karen Backstein
Genre: Fiction, Folktale; Use: Read with help

When six blind men encounter an elephant for the first time, they each have a very different impression of their experience. This retelling of a familiar folktale uses simple vocabulary and sentence structure and lovely color illustrations that will appeal to beginning readers. A wonderful book to use in a discussion of picture clues and theme.

Charlotte's Web
by E. B. White
Genre: Fiction, Fantasy; Use: Read aloud

After Wilbur the pig is raised by Mr. Zuckerman's daughter, Fern, he must live in the barn on Mr. Zuckerman's farm. There he meets Templeton the rat and Charlotte the beautiful grey spider. The farm animals soon become friends. But it is Wilbur's friendship with Charlotte, who devises a plan to save him from certain death, that is the most special of all. Students will enjoy discussing the animal characters and talking about their special friendship. Use this book to compare fantasy and reality.

The Books in the Grade 2 Library

The Emperor's New Clothes
by Hans Christian Andersen
Genre: Fiction, Fairy Tale, Classic; Use: Read aloud

Two clever thieves tell a vain emperor that they will weave the most unusual cloth in the world. There's just one catch—the cloth is invisible to anyone who is not fit for his office or who is extremely stupid. No one in the court, least of all the emperor himself, will admit to not seeing the cloth. When the emperor leads a procession through town, wearing nothing but his new, invisible clothes, one of his youngest subjects tells the truth. Colorful, detailed illustrations complement the story. Use this classic tale for a discussion of character traits.

Folktales from China
retold by Barbara Lawson
Genre: Fiction, Folktale; Use: Read aloud

This chapter book includes three folktales from China. In "The Old Man of the Steppe," a wise man recognizes both the good and bad in life, when other villagers cannot. In "Fishing for the Moon," a foolish man believes that the moon has fallen into his well. The last tale, "Two of Everything," depicts what happens when a magic brass pot that creates two of everything changes the lives of an old man and his wife. Colorful pictures illustrate the stories. This is a wonderful book for illustrating fantasy and reality.

Johnny Appleseed: A Tall Tale
by Steven Kellogg
Genre: Fiction, American Legends; Use: Read aloud

This picture book is the story of John Chapman, the American folk hero who later became known as Johnny Appleseed. The simply written text and full-page, detailed illustrations are a wonderful introduction to the life and adventures of a wanderer and nature lover who planted apple orchards throughout the American wilderness. The book is also a good introduction to American life during the late eighteenth and early nineteenth centuries. Students will enjoy comparing this book with the story of Johnny Appleseed in *American Tall Tales*. This is a great book to use in discussing character traits, story events, and picture details.

The Memory Coat
by Elvira Woodruff
Genre: Historical Fiction; Use: Read aloud

After the Cossacks sweep through their small village in Russia, young Rachel and her friend Grisha leave for America with Rachel's family. During the long, difficult journey the group worries about the inspection that awaits them at Ellis Island. When Grisha is slightly injured, Rachel devises a plan to ensure that her good friend will be able to pass the inspection with the rest of her family. This excellent introduction to the immigrants' experience at Ellis Island complements *...If Your Name Was Changed at Ellis Island*.

Paul Bunyan and Other Tall Tales
by Jane Mason
Genre: Fiction, American Legends; Use: Read aloud

This is a collection of American tall tales about some amazing legendary folk heroes, including the logger Paul Bunyan; Stormalong, the "superior sailor;" and the sharpshooting star, Annie Oakley. There is an introduction to each story that explains the background and significance of the character. This is a terrific book for discussing character traits and humor. Students will enjoy comparing the stories in this book with legends about the same characters from other books in this program. The book is not illustrated.

Pecos Bill
by Steven Kellogg
Genre: Fiction, American Legends; Use: Read aloud

This is the story of the folk hero, Pecos Bill, who was adopted by a coyote family when he was a baby and taught the ways of wild creatures. Bill went on to capture and tame the wild horse, Lightning, by bucking him across three states. Students will love these adventures of the world's greatest cowboy, including his courtship of Slewfoot Sue. The colorful pictures capture the humor and energy of the story. This is a wonderful book to use in discussing story events and character. Students will enjoy comparing Pecos Bill with some of the other folk heroes they have read about in this program.

Punctuation Takes a Vacation
by Robin Pulver
Genre: Fiction; Use: Read aloud

When Mr. Wright's students head for the playground to cool off, the abandoned punctuation marks decide to take a much needed vacation, too. Suddenly, nothing the children read makes much sense—except the many postcards from the vacationing punctuation marks. In the end, order is restored. Mr. Wright's students learn to never again take punctuation marks for granted—and neither will the readers of this enchanting book. This book makes its point about the importance of punctuation—with an exclamation mark! The acrylic illustrations are bold and fun. This is a good book for discussing humor, sequence—and punctuation.

HISTORY & GEOGRAPHY

Amelia and Eleanor Go For a Ride
by Pam Muñoz Ryan
Genre: Historical Fiction; Use: Read aloud

On April 20, 1933, Amelia Earhart arranged to take Eleanor Roosevelt for a nighttime flight over Washington, D.C. In this fictionalized account of the event, the First Lady reciprocates by taking Amelia for a ride in her new car. This book is a wonderful introduction to the lives of two great American women, both of whom spoke out for human rights. The graphite and colored pencil illustrations are terrific. Use the book to discuss character traits, plot and picture details, and to compare and contrast.

The Books in the Grade 2 Library

Clara Barton: Rookie Biographies®
by Wil Mara
Genre: Nonfiction, Biography, Historical; Use: Read aloud

This entry in the *Rookie Biography* series tells young readers about the life of Clara Barton, the founder of the American Red Cross. Students learn about Barton's work on behalf of injured soldiers during the Civil War and those wounded during the explosion of the *U.S.S. Maine* in Cuba. Nonfiction elements include phonetic respellings, photographs and period illustrations, an illustrated Words You Know section, and an index.

Harvesting Hope: The Story of Cesar Chavez
by Kathleen Krull
Genre: Nonficton, Biography; Use: Read aloud

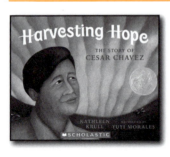

This is a biography of Cesar Chavez, the Mexican American farm worker who devoted his life to improving the working conditions of migrant workers in the United States. When he founded the National Farm Workers Association, *La Causa*—The Cause—was born. The 1965 strike against one of the forty powerful vineyard owners in California resulted in recognition of his union and the first contract for farm workers in American history. During the strike Chavez and his supporters walked 340 miles to Sacramento, the longest protest march in U.S. history. This is a wonderful introduction to an important figure in American labor history. Students will love the brightly colored, stylized illustrations as well as the stirring, real-life story.

If Not For the Cat
by Jack Prelutsky
Genre: Fiction; Use: Read aloud

Each two-page spread in this collection of haikus perfectly conveys the mood, action, or intrinsic quality of a different animal. Subjects range from a moth to bald eagles, butterflies, and an elephant. The richly colored, full-page illustrations complement the sophisticated language. This is a wonderful book for comparing and contrasting, identifying settings, and discussing figurative language and different styles of poetry.

Martin Luther King, Jr. and the March On Washington
by Francis E. Ruffin
Genre: Nonfiction, Social Studies; Use: Read aloud

Using simple text, photographs, and full-page, colorful illustrations, this book describes the famous civil rights March on Washington, D.C., which took place on August 28, 1963. The high point of the day was the historic "I Have A Dream" speech delivered by Dr. Martin Luther King, Jr. The book includes background information to place the events in historical perspective. Excerpts from the speech are also included. Compare and contrast this book with *Harvesting Hope*.

Mary McLeod Bethune: Rookie Biographies
by Susan Evento
Genre: Nonfiction, Biography, Historical; Use: Read aloud

This biography tells young readers about Mary McLeod Bethune, a civil rights leader and an advocate for women who devoted her life as an educator to opening a school for African American girls. The simple text is easy to read. Nonfiction elements include photographs, an illustrated Words You Know section, an index, and an About the Author feature.

Nettie's Trip South
by Ann Turner
Genre: Historical Fiction; Use: Read aloud

A young woman travels to the South before the Civil War and writes a letter to her sister describing her experiences there, especially her horrified reaction to a slave auction she witnessed. This book was inspired by the author's great-grandmother's trip south in 1859, an event which made her a committed abolitionist. This book could be the springboard for a class discussion about slavery in the United States. It's beautifully written and illustrated. Literary elements include author's point of view, characterization, and descriptive writing.

O, Say Can You See? America's Symbols, Landmarks, and Inspiring Words
by Sheila Keenan
Genre: Nonfiction; Use: Read aloud

This book introduces young readers to a variety of American symbols, from the Liberty Bell to our national anthem, by explaining their origin and historical significance. There are four main sections: Important Places, Interesting Objects, Inspiring Words, and Celebrating American Holidays. The book includes a glossary, index, and a list of books to read. Each two-page spread covers one topic. The pastel and colored pencil illustrations have a light-hearted tone that will appeal to students.

A Picture Book of Harriet Tubman
by David A. Adler
Genre: Nonfiction, Biography, Historical; Use: Read aloud

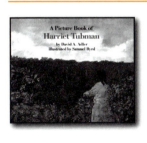

This is the story of Harriet Tubman, who escaped slavery by traveling on the Underground Railroad. After reaching a safe haven in Pennsylvania, she became a "conductor" on the Railroad. Tubman led three hundred slaves to freedom by taking them from one safe house to the next. The book includes background information about the important political issues of the period. There are full-page, color illustrations and a chronology of the key events in Tubman's life.

The Books in the Grade 2 Library

Rosa Parks: From the Back of the Bus to the Front of a Movement
by Camilla Wilson
Genre: Nonfiction, Biography, Historical; Use: Read aloud

Rosa Parks made history when she was arrested for refusing to give up her seat on a segregated Montgomery, Alabama bus. This book is the biography of the strong-willed woman who became a central figure in the civil rights movement because of her pivotal role in the Montgomery bus boycott. Nonfiction elements include a section of photographs with captions. Students can compare Rosa Parks with other civil rights figures they have read about in this program.

Teammates
by Peter Golenbock
Genre: Nonfiction, Biography, Historical; Use: Read aloud

This is the story of the friendship that developed between Jackie Robinson and Pee Wee Reese, who played for the Brooklyn Dodgers baseball team. When Robinson joined the team in 1947, he became the first black American in the Major Leagues. During a game in Cincinnati, Reese supported his teammate, who had been insulted by the crowd. Although the text is simple, it includes information about racial prejudice of the period so students can understand Robinson and Reese's achievements in the context of the times. Compare and contrast this book with stories about other civil rights heroes in this program.

True Stories About Abraham Lincoln
by Ruth Belov Gross
Genre: Nonfiction, Biography, Historical; Use: Read aloud

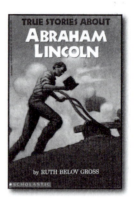

Each two-page chapter in this book includes a one-page true story about Abraham Lincoln and a full-page black-and-white woodcut illustration. The twenty two chapters present a comprehensive overview of Lincoln's life that beginning readers will easily understand. Nonfiction elements include a table of contents, chapter titles, and a brief chronology of key dates in Lincoln's life. This is a good book to compare with information about the same period in *A Picture Book of Harriet Tubman.*

Visual Arts

Henri Matisse: Getting to Know the World's Greatest Artists
by Mike Venezia
Genre: Nonfiction, Social Studies; Use: Read aloud

Another entry in this popular series for young readers, this book introduces children to the life and times of Henri Matisse, one of the most important painters of the twentieth century. Most pages include both text and illustrations. There are numerous reproductions of Matisse's work as well as humorous, cartoon-style drawings by the author.

Henri Rousseau: Getting to Know the World's Greatest Artists
by Mike Venezia
Genre: Nonfiction, Social Studies; Use: Read aloud

This is a terrific introduction to the life and times of Henri Rousseau, the French painter best known for his colorful, stylized jungle paintings. Most pages include both text and illustrations. There are numerous reproductions of Rousseau's work as well as humorous, cartoon-style drawings by the author. The text is simply written and accessible to beginning readers. Students can compare and contrast the artist's life with biographical information about other artists in this program.

Marc Chagall: Getting to Know the World's Greatest Artists
by Mike Venezia
Genre: Nonfiction, Social Studies; Use: Read aloud

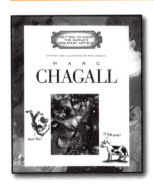

This book describes the life and work of Marc Chagall, from his birth in Russia in 1887 to his death in 1985. The simple, informative text places Chagall's life within the context of important twentieth century events that influenced him. Students will love Chagall's colorful, imaginative, and often mysterious art. The book includes numerous reproductions of his work as well as the author's signature cartoon-like drawings. Students can compare and contrast Chagall's life with information about other artists in this program.

Picasso: Getting to Know the World's Greatest Artists
by Mike Venezia
Genre: Nonfiction, Social Studies; Use: Read aloud

This is an excellent introduction to the life and times of Pablo Picasso. The text is simply written, and the book includes reproductions of Picasso's work as well as humorous cartoon-style drawings by the author. Students can compare and contrast Picasso's life with information about other artists in this popular series.

Van Gogh: Getting to Know the World's Greatest Artists
by Mike Venezia
Genre: Nonfiction, Social Studies; Use: Read aloud

This simply written biography of the nineteenth century Dutch artist Vincent van Gogh will appeal to young readers. The book includes numerous reproductions of van Gogh's work as well as the author's own colorful, cartoon-like drawings. Use this book to compare paintings by various artists. It's a terrific companion biography to other books in this series.

The Books in the Grade 2 Library

Music

Arroz Con Leche: Popular Songs and Rhymes from Latin America

selected by Lulu Delacre

Genre: Fiction, Song, Illustrated; Use: Read aloud

This wonderful collection includes twelve Latin American songs and games and rhymes from Mexico, Puerto Rico, and Argentina. Each two-page spread includes both the Spanish- and English-language versions of the text. Many of the color illustrations portray actual places or indigenous scenes that are representative of the regions. Sheet music for the songs is included. Literary elements include rhythm, rhyme, and setting.

By the Dawn's Early Light: The Story of the Star-Spangled Banner

by Steven Kroll

Genre: Nonfiction, Song, Illustrated; Use: Read aloud

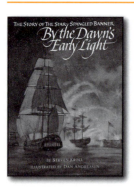

Francis Scott Key was a well-known Washington lawyer who witnessed the British attack on Fort McHenry in Baltimore, Maryland during the War of 1812. Inspired by the Americans' victory and the sight of the Stars and Stripes still flying over the fort, he wrote a poem that became the lyrics to "The Star-Spangled Banner." It became the official anthem of the United States in 1931. Each two-page spread in the book has one page of text and a full-page, color illustration. Nonfiction elements include a photograph of the original manuscript of the poem, sheet music of the anthem, maps, and an index.

Wolfgang Amadeus Mozart: Getting to Know the World's Greatest Composers

by Mike Venezia

Genre: Nonfiction, Social Studies; Use: Read with help

This is a biography of the Austrian child prodigy who wrote more than 800 musical compositions before his death at thirty-five. The numerous illustrations include photographs, paintings, as well as the author's signature, cartoon-like drawings. This book is more text heavy than others by Venezia; however, it's a good choice for discussing character.

Mathematics

The Icky Bug Counting Book

by Jerry Pallotta

Genre: Nonfiction, Science; Use: Read with help

This fact-filled counting book introduces readers to twenty-six bugs while teaching them to count from zero to twenty-six. Each page includes a beautiful color illustration of a bug and a paragraph of information. Students can discuss the pictures, talk about the text, and try to solve the riddle on the very last page. This is a great book for teaching both science and math.

Less Than Zero
by Stuart J. Murphy
Genre: Nonfiction, Numbers, Counting Book; Use: Read aloud

This entry in the MathStart® series shows students how they use math in their daily lives. In this story Perry the Penguin has to save nine clams to buy an ice scooter. There's a problem—he's not very good at managing his finances. As he earns, borrows, finds, and loses clams, Penguin keeps track on a simple line graph that demonstrates the concepts of positive and negative numbers. There are two pages of activities for adults and children that extend the math concepts presented in the book.

Math Fables: Lessons That Count
by Greg Tang
Genre: Nonfiction, Rhyme; Use: Read with help

The rhyming fables in this book begin by introducing numbers in a traditional way that is familiar to students—by counting. However, as the stories progress, students learn to think about numbers in different ways by grouping them. For example, a tale about six playful otters shows students how to group the number 6 as 4 and 2, 5 and 1, and two groups of 3 each. The book concludes with a page of math activities to help children become more fluent with numbers. Literary elements include rhythm and rhyme.

Math for All Seasons: Mind-Stretching Math Riddles
by Greg Tang
Genre: Nonfiction, Rhyme, Rhyming Story; Use: Read with help

Each two-page spread in this book includes rhyming text and a full-page illustration to teach problem solving. By asking students to figure out the solution to a problem, such as "How many plants are still in bloom?" the text "introduces intuitive ways to group and add numbers." Each verse includes a clue to help students figure out the answer. Literary elements include rhythm and rhyme.

One Hundred Ways to Get to 100
by Jerry Pallotta
Genre: Nonfiction, Numbers, Counting Book; Use: Read with help

This book demonstrates that there are at least one hundred ways to count to one hundred. As students progress through the text, they add by ones and by equal groups; they also multiply, subtract, and divide. Each computation involves objects that are familiar to students—from pencils to toothbrushes. The simply written text shows just how interesting counting can be.

The Books in the Grade 2 Library

Only One
by Marc Harshman
Genre: Fiction, Number, Counting Book; **Use:** Read with help

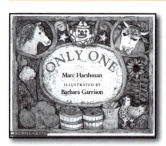

Students will love this enchanting visit to a country fair where they are invited to count all kinds of things in the colorful pictures, including the bees in one hive and the seeds in one pumpkin. Each page reinforces the concept that all the people and items they count still make up one whole. When they're finished reading and counting, students will enjoy finding other things to count in their classroom and school.

Science

Back and Forth: Rookie Read-About® Science
by Patricia J. Murphy
Genre: Nonfiction, Science; **Use:** Read alone

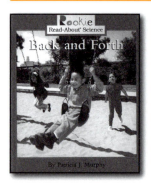

This *Rookie Read-About Science* book introduces students to the concept of backward and forward motion. Colorful photos and simple text encourage students to read on their own and find out how these forces are used in everyday life. Nonfiction features include labeled photographs that illustrate key words, phonetic respellings, and an index.

Chickens Aren't the Only Ones
by Ruth Heller
Genre: Nonfiction, Science; **Use:** Read with help

Young readers will be surprised to find out the different kinds of animals that lay eggs. As this beautifully illustrated book points out—chickens aren't the only ones. Reptiles, amphibians, large and small fish, insects, and even two kinds of mammals lay eggs too. The simple text includes some rhyme. The richly detailed pictures provide a springboard for classroom discussion.

The Digestive System: A True Book
by Darlene R. Stille
Genre: Nonfiction, Science; **Use:** Read aloud

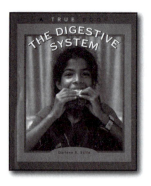

This book is an excellent introduction to the different parts of the human digestive system and how each part functions. The book has information on a variety of topics, including what happens when someone swallows food, organs that help with digestion, and the link between digestion and health. The short chapters are simply written but very informative. Numerous full-color photographs and detailed captions are helpful in understanding the text. Other nonfiction elements include chapter headings, a section with important words, an index, a Meet the Author page, and a list of supplemental books, organizations, and Internet sites.

Experiments With Magnets: A True Book
by Salvatore Tocci
Genre: Nonfiction, Science; Use: Read aloud

This chapter book about magnets includes eight simple experiments that can be performed by students working in pairs or small groups. Topics include making electricity, finding the earth's poles, attracting metals, and performing magic. The activities are well illustrated and include a list of materials. Nonfiction elements include a table of contents, a glossary, an index, and bibliographical references. Students can discuss or record their observations for future reference.

Forces Around Us
by Sally Hewitt
Genre: Nonfiction, Science; Use: Read aloud

This book uses an interactive approach to introduce the concept of force and to discuss a variety of forces that children encounter in their everyday world, such as gravity, magnetism, and weight. Each two-page spread focuses on one topic and includes different kinds of activities that encourage young readers to think, talk about, and explore new ideas for themselves. The simple text is enhanced by the color photographs that feature children. Other nonfiction elements include a glossary and an index. This is a great book to use in discussing students' observations about the physical world.

Frog and Toad All Year
by Arnold Lobel
Genre: Fiction, Early Chapter Book; Use: Read alone

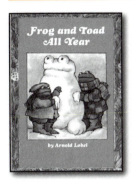

Students will love the five funny stories about best friends, Frog and Toad. Each of the tales takes place in a different season of the year. Whether they are playing in the snow, eating ice cream on a hot summer day, or spending Christmas Eve together, it's easy to see why Frog and Toad are the best of friends. Children will learn about the seasons as they follow the adventures of Frog and Toad. Students will enjoy this classic beginning chapter book.

Frog and Toad Are Friends
by Arnold Lobel
Genre: Fiction, Early Chapter Book; Use: Read alone

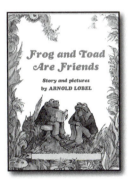

Like the other books in this series, each chapter tells a different story about Frog and Toad. When Frog is sick in bed, it's his best friend who helps him. And when Toad thinks he's lost a button, it's his best friend who helps him too. Children will learn life lessons from the spare text and lovely, softly colored illustrations. Students will enjoy retelling the stories in their own words and talking about the animal characters.

The Books in the Grade 2 Library

From Caterpillar to Butterfly
by Dr. Gerald Legg
Genre: Nonfiction; Use: Read aloud

This *Lifecycles* book focuses on the development of a caterpillar into a butterfly. The simple text is complemented by full-page, color illustrations that record each stage in the process. These detailed pictures are a wonderful starting point for class discussion. Other nonfiction elements include labels, captions, a table of contents, an information section, a glossary, and an index.

From Egg to Chicken
by Dr. Gerald Legg
Genre: Nonfiction, Science; Use: Read aloud

Using simple text and large color illustrations, this book describes the life cycle of a chicken, from the development of the embryo to the hatching of the egg, and the growth of a chick into a mature bird. The illustrations are richly detailed and include labels and captions. Other nonfiction elements include a glossary, an index, and a table of contents. This book is appropriate for identifying steps in a process and discussing picture clues. Use it also to encourage independent research activities.

From Seed to Sunflower
by Dr. Gerald Legg
Genre: Nonfiction, Science; Use: Read aloud

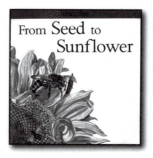

This *Lifecycles* book explains how a seed develops into a sunflower. The simple text is accompanied by full-page, color illustrations that record each stage in the process. Topics includes germination, roots and shoots, buds, and pollination. The detailed pictures are a wonderful starting point for class discussion. Other nonfiction elements include labels, captions, a table of contents, an information section with sunflower facts, a glossary, and an index. This book illustrates steps in a process for beginning readers.

From Tadpole to Frog
by David Steward
Genre: Nonfiction, Science; Use: Read aloud

This *Lifecycles* book explains how a tadpole develops into a frog. The simple text is complemented by full-page, color illustrations that record each stage in the process. Topics discussed in the two-page chapters include: what is a frog; how they spawn; and where and how tadpoles develop. The detailed pictures are a wonderful starting point for class discussion. Other nonfiction elements include labels, captions, a table of contents, an information section with frog facts, a glossary, and an index. This book illustrates steps in a process for beginning readers. Students can compare the life cycle of a frog with the life cycle of other animals studied in this program.

Insects & Spiders: Worldwise

by Penny Clarke
Genre: Nonfiction, Science; **Use:** Read aloud

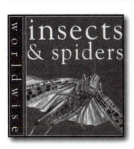

Each two-page chapter describes the physical characteristics, life cycles, and natural habitats of a variety of insects. The simple text is supplemented by colorful full-page illustrations with informative labels and captions. Other nonfiction elements include a table of contents, a glossary, and an index. The illustrations are so detailed that they can be used as a springboard for a discussion or an art extension activity.

The Life and Times of the Ant

by Charles Micucci
Genre: Nonfiction, Science; **Use:** Read aloud

Each of the fourteen chapters in this book presents information about a topic relating to the life and times of ants. Students learn about where ants live, how they communicate, and what they do to preserve rainforests. The two-page chapters include one paragraph of simple text and illustrations with captions and labels. Students can use this book to compare and contrast ants with some of the other insects they have read about in the program.

Magnets

by Anne Schreiber
Genre: Nonfiction, Science; **Use:** Read aloud

This book discusses the properties of magnets and explains how magnetic force affects our daily lives. The simple text and colorful drawings, featuring school-age and animal characters, will appeal to young readers. It includes several simple activities that students can try. Nonfiction elements include section headings, captions, labels, and a glossary.

1001 Bugs to Spot

by Emma Helbrough
Genre: Nonfiction, Science; **Use:** Read alone

Kids will love finding, counting, and talking about the 1001 bugs that fill the pages of this wonderful picture book. Each two-page spread illustrates a different animal habitat, from a leafy woodland to a jungle floor, where bugs fly, creep, crawl, and whirl. Use this book as the springboard for additional research, art, and writing activities.

The Books in the Grade 2 Library

Push and Pull: Rookie Read-About Science
by Patricia J. Murphy
Genre: Nonfiction, Science; **Use:** Read alone

This *Rookie Read-About Science* book introduces students to the concepts of pushing and pulling. Colorful photographs and simple text help students learn about these forces and how they affect the movement of different objects. Nonfiction features include labeled photographs that illustrate key words, phonetic respellings, and an index.

Seasons: Cycles of Life
by David Stewart
Genre: Nonfiction, Science; **Use:** Read aloud

This simply written, easy-to-read chapter book explains how the seasonal cycles affect both plant and animal life. The beautifully detailed, time-lapse illustrations use a split-page format to show the cycle of the seasons. These pictures can be a springboard for classroom discussion about the effects of seasonal changes on the countryside. Nonfiction elements include a table of contents, labels, captions, bold-faced print, and an index.

Simple Machines: Rookie Read-About Science
by Allan Fowler
Genre: Nonfiction, Science; **Use:** Read alone

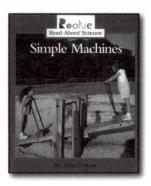

This entry in the *Rookie Read-About Science* series discusses simple machines and their use in our daily lives. The easy-to-read text and colorful photographs encourage students to identify different kinds of simple machines, such as levers, inclined planes, wheels, and pulleys. Nonfiction features include phonetic respellings, captions, labels and an index. This book will help students identify types of simple machines in their classroom and homes.

What Is a Plane? Welcome Books™
by Lloyd G. Douglass
Genre: Nonfiction, Science; **Use:** Read alone

This beginning chapter book describes a simple machine, called a plane, and variations, such as ramps and slides, that are found in students' immediate environment. Using very simple text and full-page color photographs, the book explains how these simple machines make work easier. Other nonfiction elements include a table of contents, a glossary, and an index. Use this book to help students identify main ideas and supporting details.

What Is a Pulley? Welcome Books
by Lloyd G. Douglas
Genre: Nonfiction, Science; Use: Read alone

This entry in the *Welcome Books* series explains what pulleys are and how they are used to make work easier by moving heavy objects. Each two-page spread includes minimal text and a full-page color photograph that relates to students' environment. Other nonfiction elements include chapter titles, recommended books and websites, and a glossary. Use this book to compare and contrast the simple machines described in *What Is a Pulley?* and *What Is a Plane?*

What Is a Screw? Welcome Books
by Lloyd G. Douglas
Genre: Nonfiction, Science; Use: Read alone

This book uses very simple text and full-page color photographs to explain what a screw is and how screws are used. Like the other books in this series, it introduces beginning readers to a simple machine that has many uses in their immediate environment. Nonfiction elements include a glossary, an index, and an About the Author feature. Use this book in classroom activities that require students to identify different uses of screws, planes, and pulleys in their schools or communities.

What Is Friction? Rookie Read-About Science
by Lisa Trumbauer
Genre: Nonfiction, Science; Use: Read aloud

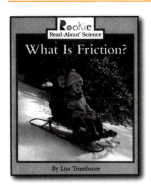

This entry in the *Rookie Read-About Science* series explains what friction is and how it affects our daily lives. The text is easy to read and the accompanying colorful photographs illustrate the concepts discussed. Students will be encouraged to read on their own as they discover how friction makes everyday objects slow down and stop. Nonfiction features include an illustrated Words You Know section, and an index.

You and Your Body: It's Science!
by Sally Hewitt
Genre: Nonfiction, Science; Use: Read aloud

Each two-page chapter presents information about a different topic that helps students better understand their bodies and how to stay healthy. From naming the parts of the body to the importance of sleeping well, children learn important facts about anatomy and physiology. Special features in each chapter provide an interactive link with the material. Nonfiction elements include full-page color photographs, diagrams, words in boldface, a glossary of useful words, and an index.

The Books in the Grade 2 Library

You Can Use a Balance: Rookie Read-About Science
by Linda Bullock
Genre: Nonfiction, Science; Use: Read alone

This entry in the easy-to-read series introduces students to many different kinds of balances and explains how they are used in our daily lives. Colorful photos illustrate the concepts discussed in the text. Nonfiction elements include phonetic respellings, an illustrated Words You Know section, and an index.

You Can Use a Compass: Rookie Read-About Science
by Lisa Trumbauer
Genre: Nonfiction, Science; Use: Read alone

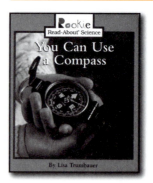

Using simple text and color photographs, this entry in the series explains what a compass is and how it is used to find one's way on land, at sea, or in the air. Useful nonfiction elements include phonetic respellings of difficult words, an illustrated Words You Know section, and an index. Use this book to reinforce students' understanding of map directions.

Book Cover Credits

Language Arts/English

The Blind Men and the Elephant by Karen Backstein, illustrated by Annie Mitra. Illustrations copyright © 1992 by Annie Mitra. Published by Scholastic Inc. All rights reserved.

Charlotte's Web by E. B. White, illustrated by Garth Williams. Copyright © 1952 by E. B. White. Published by Scholastic Inc. by arrangement with HarperCollins Publishers. All rights reserved.

The Emperor's New Clothes by Hans Christian Andersen, illustrated by Pamela Baldwin Ford. Copyright © 1979 by Scholastic Inc. Published by Scholastic Inc. All rights reserved.

Folktales from China by Barbara Lawson, illustrated by Kristina Swarner. Copyright © 2002 by Scholastic Inc. Published by Scholastic Inc. All rights reserved.

Johnny Appleseed retold and illustrated by Steven Kellogg. Copyright © 1988 by Steven Kellogg. Published by Scholastic Inc. All rights reserved.

The Memory Coat by Elvira Woodruff, illustrated by Michael Dooling. Illustrations copyright © 1999 by Michael Dooling. Published by Scholastic Inc. All rights reserved.

Paul Bunyan and Other Tall Tales, adapted by Jane Mason. Copyright © 2002 by Jane Mason. Published by Scholastic Inc. All rights reserved. Cover illustration by James Bernardin.

Pecos Bill by Steven Kellogg. Copyright © 1986 by Steven Kellogg. Published by Scholastic Inc. by arrangement with HarperCollins Publishers. All rights reserved.

Punctuation Takes a Vacation by Robin Pulver, illustrated by Lynn Rowe Reed. Illustrations copyright © 2003 by Lynn Rowe Reed. Published by Scholastic Inc. by arrangement with Holiday house, Inc. All rights reserved.

History & Geography

Amelia and Eleanor Go for a Ride by Pam Muñoz Ryan, illustrated by Brian Selznick. Illustrations copyright © 1999 by Brian Selznick. Published by Scholastic Inc. All rights reserved.

Clara Barton by Wil Mara. Copyright © 2002 by Children's Press. Published by Children's Press, a division of Scholastic Inc. All rights reserved. Cover: Brown Brothers.

Harvesting Hope: The Story of Cesar Chavez by Kathleen Krull, illustrated by Yuyi Morales. Illustrations copyright © 2003 by Yuyi Morales. Published by Scholastic Inc. by arrangement with Harcourt, Inc. All rights reserved.

If Not for the Cat by Jack Prelutsky, paintings by Ted Rand. Illustrations copyright © 2004 by Ted Rand. Published by Scholastic Inc. by arrangement with HarperCollins Publishers. All rights reserved.

Martin Luther King, Jr. and the March on Washington by Frances E. Ruffin, illustrated by Stephen Marchesi. Illustrations copyright © 2001 by Stephen Marchesi. Published by Scholastic Inc. by arrangement with Penguin Putnam Books for Young Readers, a division of Penguin Group (USA) Inc. All rights reserved.

Mary McLeod Bethune by Susan Evento. Copyright © 2004 by Scholastic Inc. Published by Children's Press, a division of Scholastic Inc. All rights reserved. Cover: Florida State Archives.

Book Cover Credits

NETTIE'S TRIP SOUTH by Ann Turner, illustrated by Ronald Himler. Illustrations copyright © 1987 by Ronald Himler. Published by Scholastic Inc. by arrangement with Simon & Schuster Children's Publishing Division. All rights reserved.

O, SAY CAN YOU SEE? AMERICA'S SYMBOLS, LANDMARKS, AND IMPORTANT WORDS by Sheila Keenan, illustrated by Ann Boyajian. Illustrations copyright © 2004 by Ann Boyajian. Published by Scholastic Inc. All rights reserved.

A PICTURE BOOK OF HARRIET TUBMAN by David A. Adler, illustrated by Samuel Byrd. Illustrations copyright © 1992 by Samuel Byrd. Published by Holiday House, Inc. All rights reserved.

ROSA PARKS: FROM THE BACK OF THE BUS TO THE FRONT OF A MOVEMENT by Camilla Wilson. Copyright © 2001 by Camilla Wilson. Published by Scholastic Inc. All rights reserved.

TEAMMATES by Peter Golenbock, illustrated by Paul Bacon. Illustrations copyright © 1990 by Paul Bacon. Published by Scholastic Inc. by arrangement with Harcourt, Inc. All rights reserved.

TRUE STORIES ABOUT ABRAHAM LINCOLN by Ruth Belov Gross, illustrated by Charles Turzak. Copyright © 1973 by Ruth Belov Gross. Published by Scholastic Inc. All rights reserved.

Visual Arts

HENRI MATISSE by Mike Venezia. Copyright © 1997 by Mike Venezia. Published by Children's Press, a division of Scholastic Inc. All rights reserved. Cover: *Horse Rider and Clown* from the portfolio *Jazz* by Henri Matisse, Museum of Modern Art, New York, Gift of the Artist.

HENRI ROUSSEAU by Mike Venezia. Copyright © 2002 by Mike Venezia. Published by Children's Press, a division of Scholastic Inc. All rights reserved. Cover: *Fight of a Tiger and Buffalo* by Henri Rousseau, 1949, Cleveland Museum of Art, Gift of the Hanna Fund.

MARC CHAGALL by Mike Venezia. Copyright © 2000 by Mike Venezia. Published by Children's Press, a division of Scholastic Inc. All rights reserved. Cover: *I and the Village* by Marc Chagall, Museum of Modern Art, New York, Mrs. Simon Guggenheim Fund.

PICASSO by Mike Venezia. Copyright © 1998 by Regensteiner Publishing Enterprises, Inc. Published by Children's Press, a division of Scholastic Inc. All rights reserved. Cover: *Boy in Sailor Suit with Butterfly Net* by Pablo Picasso, 1938, Phototheque, SPADEM/Art Resource.

VAN GOGH by Mike Venezia. Copyright © 1998 by Regensteiner Publishing Enterprises, Inc. Published by Children's Press, a division of Scholastic Inc. All rights reserved. Cover: *Olive Trees* by Vincent Van Gogh, 1889, The Minneapolis Institute of Arts.

Music

ARROZ CON LECHE: POPULAR SONGS AND RHYMES FROM LATIN AMERICAN, selected and illustrated by Lulu Delacre. Copyright © 1989 by Lulu Delacre. Published by Scholastic Inc. All rights reserved.

BY THE DAWN'S EARLY LIGHT: THE STORY OF STAR-SPANGLED BANNER by Steven Kroll, illustrated by Dan Andreasen. Illustrations copyright © 1994 by Dan Andreasen. Published by Scholastic Inc. All rights reserved.

WOLFGANG AMADEUS MOZART by Mike Venezia. Copyright © 1995 by Mike Venezia. Published by Children's Press, a division of Scholastic Inc. All rights reserved. Cover: Stock Montage, Inc.

Mathematics

Icky Bug Numbers 1 2 3 by Jerry Pallotta, illustrated by David Biedrzycki and Rob Bolster. Illustrations copyright © 2003 by David Biedrzycki and Rob Bolster. Published by Scholastic Inc. All rights reserved.

Less Than Zero by Stuart J. Murphy, illustrated by Frank Remkiewcz. Illustrations copyright © 2003 by Frank Remkiewcz. Published by Scholastic Inc. by arrangement with HarperCollins Publishers. All rights reserved.

Math Fables by Greg Tang, illustrated by Heather Cahoon. Text and illustrations copyright © 2004 by Gregory Tang. Published by Scholastic Inc. All rights reserved.

Math for All Seasons by Greg Tang, illustrated by Harry Briggs. Text and illustrations copyright © 2002 by Gregory Tang. Published by Scholastic Inc. All rights reserved.

One Hundred Ways to Get to 100 by Jerry Pallotta, illustrated by Rob Bolster. Illustrations copyright © 2003 by Rob Bolster. Published by Scholastic Inc. All rights reserved.

Only One by Marc Harshman, illustrated by Barbara Garrison. Illustrations copyright © 1993 by Barbara Garrison. Published by Scholastic Inc. by arrangement with Penguin Putnam Books for Young Readers, a division of Penguin Group (USA) Inc. All rights reserved.

Science

1001 Bugs to Spot by Emma Helbrough, illustrated by Teri Gower. Copyright © 2005 by Usborne Publishing Ltd. Published by Scholastic Inc. by arrangement with Usborne Publishing Ltd. All rights reserved.

Back and Forth by Patricia J. Murphy. Copyright © 2002 by Children's Press. Published by Children's Press, a division of Scholastic Inc. All rights reserved. Cover: Michael Newman/PhotoEdit.

Chickens Aren't the Only Ones by Ruth Heller. Copyright © 1991 by Ruth Heller. Published by Scholastic Inc. by arrangement with Penguin Putnam Books for Young Readers, a division of Penguin Group (USA) Inc. All rights reserved.

The Digestive System by Darlene R. Stille. Copyright © 1997 by Children's Press. Published by Children's Press, a division of Scholastic Inc. All rights reserved. Cover: Young-Wolff/PhotoEdit.

Experiments with Magnets by Salvatore Tocci. Copyright © 2001 by Children's Press. Published by Children's Press, a division of Scholastic Inc. All rights reserved. Cover: Richard Megna/Fundamental Photos.

Forces Around Us by Sally Hewitt. Copyright © 1997 by Franklin Watts. Published by Franklin Watts, a division of Scholastic Inc. All rights reserved.

Frog and Toad All Year by Arnold Lobel. Copyright © 1976 by Arnold Lobel. Published by Scholastic Inc. by arrangement with HarperCollins Publishers. All rights reserved.

Frog and Toad Are Friends by Arnold Lobel. Copyright © 1970 by Arnold Lobel. Published by Scholastic Inc. by arrangement with HarperCollins Publishers. All rights reserved.

From Caterpillar to Butterfly by Dr. Gerald Legg, illustrated by Carolyn Scrace. Copyright © 1997 The Salariya Book Company Ltd. Published by Franklin Watts, a division of Scholastic Inc. All rights reserved.

Book Cover Credits

FROM EGG TO CHICKEN by Gerald Legg, illustrated by Carolyn Scrace. Copyright © 1997 by The Salariya Book Company, Ltd. Published by Franklin Watts, a division of Scholastic Inc. All rights reserved.

FROM SEED TO SUNFLOWER by Gerald Legg, illustrated by Carolyn Scrace. Copyright © 1997 The Salariya Book Company Ltd. Published by Franklin Watts, a division of Scholastic Inc. All rights reserved.

FROM TADPOLE TO FROG by Gerald Legg, illustrated by Carolyn Scrace. Copyright © 1997 The Salariya Book Company Ltd. Published by Franklin Watts, a division of Scholastic Inc. All rights reserved.

INSECTS & SPIDERS by Penny Clarke, illustrated by Carolyn Scrace. Copyright © 1995 The Salariya Book Company Ltd. Published by Franklin Watts, a division of Scholastic Inc. All rights reserved.

THE LIFE AND TIMES OF THE ANT by Charles Micucci. Copyright © 2003 by Charles Micucci. Published by Scholastic Inc. by arrangement with Houghton Mifflin Company. All rights reserved.

MAGNETS by Anne Schreiber, illustrated by Adrian C. Sinnott. Illustrations copyright © 2003 by Adrian C. Sinnott. Published by Scholastic Inc. by arrangement with Penguin Putnam Books for Young Readers, a division of Penguin Group (USA) Inc. All rights reserved.

PUSH AND PULL by Patricia J. Murphy. Copyright © 2002 by Children's Press. Published by Children's Press, a division of Scholastic Inc. All rights reserved. Cover: Barbara Stitzer/PhotoEdit.

SEASONS by David Stewart, illustrated by Alan Baker. Copyright © 2002 The Salariya Book Company Ltd. Published by Franklin Watts, a division of Scholastic Inc. All rights reserved.

SIMPLE MACHINES by Allan Fowler. Copyright © 2001 by Children's Press. Published by Children's Press, a division of Scholastic Inc. All rights reserved. Cover: Nance S. Trueworthy.

WHAT IS A PLANE? by Lloyd G. Douglas. Copyright © 2002 by Rosen Book Works, Inc. Published by Children's Press, a division of Scholastic Inc. All rights reserved. Cover: Maura B. McConnell.

WHAT IS A PULLEY? by Lloyd G. Douglas. Copyright © 2002 by Rosen Book Works, Inc. Published by Children's Press, a division of Scholastic Inc. All rights reserved. Cover: Cindy Reiman.

WHAT IS A SCREW? by Lloyd G. Douglas. Copyright © 2002 by Rosen Book Works, Inc. Published by Children's Press, a division of Scholastic Inc. All rights reserved. Cover: Cindy Reiman.

WHAT IS FRICTION? by Lisa Trumbauer. Copyright © 2004 by Scholastic Inc. Published by Children's Press, a division of Scholastic Inc. All rights reserved. Cover: David Young-Wolff/PhotoEdit.

YOU AND YOUR BODY by Sally Hewitt. Copyright © 1998 by Franklin Watts. Published by Franklin Watts, a division of Scholastic Inc. All rights reserved. Cover: Franklin Watts.

YOU CAN USE A BALANCE by Linda Bullock. Copyright © 2003 by Scholastic Inc. Published by Children's Press, a division of Scholastic Inc. All rights reserved. Cover: Randy Matusow/PhotoEdit.

YOU CAN USE A COMPASS by Lisa Trumbauer. Copyright © 2003 by Scholastic Inc. Published by Children's Press, a division of Scholastic Inc. All rights reserved. Cover: Roger Ressmeyer/Corbis Images.